DAME FANNY WATERMAN PIANO TREASURY

VOLUME TWO

Piano repertoire for teaching and performance

FABER *ff* MUSIC

CONTENTS

FOREWORD

This Piano Treasury contains my own choices of many of the pieces which I have enjoyed teaching to pianists of all ages. I hope that this collection will help to stimulate imaginative performances.

The pieces in this publication have been favourites of, and included in the programmes performed by the Great Masters such as Rubinstein and Horowitz. All pianists should strive to make the piano sing and to capture the range of styles and timbres of the great composers: for example, the lyrical melody of Field's *Nocturne* and the serenity of Schumann's *Träumerei*; the lilt of Chopin's waltz and the variety of moods in the gaiety of Mozart's *Theme and Twelve Variations*; the violin-like sonority of the light-hearted finale from Haydn's *Sonata in F* and the simple nobility of the slow movement of Beethoven's *Pathétique Sonata*. Teachers should try to stimulate their pupils with the use of pictorial language to help with performances of Debussy's *La fille aux cheveux de lin*. I do believe that every piano lesson should be a 'musical injection' to open the pianist's mind to the gems and beauty of the composer's genius.

Teachers should encourage pianists to attend recitals as well as listening to recordings, and also to explore other genres by the composers they are studying to broaden their knowledge and experience. Remember, Beethoven's sonatas can be regarded as symphonies for the piano, with all the knowledge of the orchestration.

All teachers are privileged to teach their pupils, as Clifford Curzon so beautifully expressed in a letter to me: 'What greater pleasure in life is there than giving a young and beautiful talent a little lift in the direction of the stars, though he may never reach them.'

Dame Fanny Waterman

Notes on the music

Partita No.1 BWV 825 (JS Bach)
Bach came from a very musical family, learning the violin, harpsichord and clavichord as a child. This is the first Partita in his *Clavierübung* ('keyboard tutor'). The balance is important in the **Prelude** – work on the two parts in the left hand, finding the hidden melody. Be aware of the sonorities of the different registers of the piano and effect of the conjunct and disjunct intervals in the melody (see *Piano Lessons* Book 3, page 17 for more on this). You need to become an acrobat in the **Gigue**, with your left hand skipping above the right hand: practise this movement so your hand can move directly and accurately. This opened Rachmaninoff's recital at Leeds Town Hall when I was eight years old.

Allegro in A (CPE Bach)
CPE Bach, the fifth child of JS Bach, intended to pursue a legal career but changed to music whilst at university. He wrote over 200 keyboard sonatas, of which this is a relatively little-known but very beautiful example. Practise the piece without the ornaments at first, but do use the correct fingering so they can be added easily later on. You should always play the repeats, making sure you vary your interpretation of the music on the repetition.

Sonata in F Hob 16 No.23, Finale (Haydn)
Haydn was born in Austria and showed early signs of musical precocity. He went on to work for 30 years as Kapellmeister (director of music) to the Esterhazy household in Hungary. In this piece it is very important to play the opening two bars with the correct phrasing: it is a key facet of the sense of humour which pervades all Haydn sonatas. Try to imitate the sonority of a bowed violin in the slurred phrases, and the pizzicato articulation of the staccato notes. The pulse and tempo are important: if it is too laboured you won't capture the sense of humour, and if it is too fast it becomes a scramble. The semiquavers in particular require a *presto* brilliance: practise them by breaking up (see *Piano Lessons* Book 2 page 10 for help with this).

Theme and Twelve Variations KV 265 (Mozart)

Born in Austria, Mozart was a child prodigy and played the violin, viola and keyboard. He based this piece on a French folk song which has since become known as *Twinkle Twinkle Little Star*. The repeats are essential for variety.

Variation 1: Balance your left hand against the melodic semiquavers of the right hand (there are more notes in the right hand so the left can sing out a little more).

2: Make sure you capture the brilliance of the semiquavers in this left-hand variation. The overlapping tied notes in the right hand will need careful practice.

3: In this contrasting variation you will need to capture the *cantabile* sonority in your right hand. Fit the trills in the correct time spots.

4: This time we have triplets in the left hand – watch the rhythm and remember the importance of the second beat.

5: This *scherzando* variation has notes passed playfully between the hands: keep them separate.

6: Here the theme is established once more, combining a dignified right hand with playful left-hand semiquavers.

7: In this variation the left hand comes into its own, and at times there is a feeling of a conversation between the hands. Vary your touch according to the direction of the runs – ascending could for example be *brio*, and descending could have brilliance.

8: Introduce this minor variation a microsecond slower to capture the more sombre mood and beautiful overlapping tied notes. Notice the differing length of phrases between the hands.

9: Here we have tied notes with a new dotted rhythm – keep it crisp to avoid becoming pedestrian.

10: This variation features skipping notes in the left hand, as we had in the *Gigue* of the Bach *Prelude*.

11: This *Adagio* variation has a serious start but the mood changes after the first double bar. The *staccato* notes and descending couplets could be more graceful than humorous.

12: The final extended variation has brilliant semiquavers and a grand ending. Isolate the thumb notes at bar 30 (the first of each group of four) and practise them separately. The remaining notes will then fit in naturally.

Pathétique Sonata Op.13 No.8, second movement (Beethoven)

Ludwig van Beethoven, the German composer and pianist, is regarded as one of the most influential and reactionary composers ever. This slow movement is almost hymnal in tone – with a mood of resignation and reminiscence. Be aware of the different melodies in the right and left hands, the balance between them and the beauty of the conjunct and disjunct intervals (see *Piano Lessons* Book 3, page 17). Note the greater dynamic range in the middle section and the *fp* markings (a trademark of Beethoven). Consider the ending carefully – the three *rinforzando* phrases should each be different, before relaxing on the last chords. Leave the keys with reluctance, at the same tempo as the piece. As Menuhin said: 'Approach every note with anticipation, and leave it with regret.' (See *On Piano Teaching And Performing*.)

Nocturne No.4 in A H.36 (Field)

The Irish composer and pianist John Field was born in Dublin but moved to London to study with Clementi. Field had a distinctive style which featured beautiful simplicity and lyrical melodies. This nocturne (a piece of music inspired by both the serenity and the tensions of the night) should be played with great lyricism – your right hand should sound like a beautiful soprano. The balance is crucial: be aware of the hidden melody in the left hand at the start, dropping onto the fifth finger with a loose wrist and a dab of pedal. The demisemiquavers should be liquid in their fluidity; practise them by breaking up these groups (see *Piano Lessons* Book 2, page 10). As Tobias Matthay said 'Rhythm should be bent but never broken'.

Scherzo in B flat D.593 (Schubert)

Schubert was born in Vienna to a large family, and many of his early compositions were for the family string quartet in which he played viola. Scherzo is Italian for 'joke', indicating a light-hearted, humorous piece. This scherzo sounds simple but is deceptively tricky because of the lack of notes! The gentle anacrusis triplet opening is a hallmark of the piece. You must use more tonal colours than the six basic dynamics (*pp* to *ff*) to capture the different moods you wish to convey. Knowledge of Schubert's Lieder, string quartets and the great C major Symphony will help you to understand and appreciate both the joys and the sufferings of Schubert's masterpieces.

Waltz in B minor Op.69 No.2 (Chopin)

Chopin started writing waltzes at the age of 14 and carried on right through his life. He moved away from writing traditional Viennese waltzes to accompany dancing and developed the style, creating concert pieces for performance. Many of his major works contain strong rhythmic waltz rhythms. The anacrusis opening phrase is beautifully constructed and repeated many times: vary each phrase so it is never exactly the same (try different emphasis, quality of tone, mood, dynamics and *rubato*). Be careful with the left-hand pattern: slur from the first to go up on the second and down on the third beat of each bar. The modulation to B major is a magical moment: play it with great tenderness.

Nocturne in E flat Op.9 No.2 (Chopin)

A nocturne is a piece of music inspired by the night. Chopin didn't invent the nocturne – the Irish composer John Field wrote the first Romantic nocturnes for solo piano – but he did develop and popularise the style. A nocturne is flowing and lyrical, often featuring a broken-chord left-hand accompaniment. Treat the right hand as the singer and the left hand as the accompanist. Try starting the trills tentatively – all phrases have a rhythmical swing of beginnings and endings and emerge one from the other. Hold the pedal through the cadenza so there is an accumulation of notes, starting confidently but dropping down before the *crescendo*. The ending is calm: play the last chords as softly as you can.

Träumerei from Kinderszenen Op.15 (Schumann)

Schumann's *Kinderszenen* is made up of 12 short pieces. I recommend you listen to Horowitz's recording of *Träumerei* (meaning 'reverie' or 'dreaming') with which he moved his audience to tears at the end of his recitals, to help you capture the intense yet pensive feel of this beautiful work. Let the sound linger on until the silence fades. As Schnabel said: 'The notes I handle no better than many pianists. But the pauses between the notes—ah, that is where the art resides.' Think about this dictum, they are words of great musical wisdom! Before developing the volume or dying away at the end, do bear in mind Menuhin's comment regarding barlines – 'they are a great danger and too often represent prison bars' – I feel it is particularly appropriate to this piece. By the time you reach the last bars, there shouldn't be a dry eye in the house.

Spring Song from Songs Without Words Op.62 No.6 (Mendelssohn)

The Romantic composer Felix Mendelssohn's (one of Queen Victoria's favourite composers) best-known works for piano are the series of pieces entitled 'Songs Without Words'. Written between 1829 and 1845, these are short, lyrical, song-like pieces. In this beautiful work, spring has arrived and there is a feeling of optimism. Perform it as if your heart is lifting: as in Wordsworth's poem *Daffodils*:

> 'And then my heart with pleasure fills,
> And dances with the daffodils.'

Let the music capture your feelings on seeing the arrival of the first snowdrop.

Kinderstücke No.2 Op.72 (Mendelssohn)

Felix Mendelssohn was born into a well-to-do, intellectual family and was recognised as a musical prodigy early in life. During his short life he toured around Europe, becoming famous as a conductor, pianist and composer. *Kinderstücke* means 'children's pieces' – this piece has a rich, warm tone in E flat major. Mendelssohn employs an Alberti bass-type accompaniment and rich voicing in the right hand which complements the key. Don't forget the pause over the final rest.

October (Autumn Song) from The Seasons Op.37b (Tchaikovsky)

The Russian composer Tchaikovsky composed *The Seasons* as a commission for 12 short piano pieces, one to be published each month in a St Petersburg magazine in 1876. These character pieces are miniatures notable for their beautiful melodies. *October [Autumn Song]* is very romantic yet also extrovert and dramatic. When you are studying this piece you should imagine it is a theme from one of Tchaikovsky's symphonies – try to imitate the rich string writing in the beautiful melodic lines. The words of Keats in his poem 'To Autumn' should inspire us when we play this music:

> 'Season of mists and mellow fruitfulness…'

La fille aux cheveux de lin (Debussy)

La fille aux cheveux de lin translates roughly as 'The girl with the flaxen hair' and is one of Debussy's most famous pieces. It is from his *Préludes* Book 1, in which Debussy deliberately placed the titles at the end of the pieces because he wanted people to respond intuitively to the music rather than to be influenced by the titles. This spellbinding piece depends upon the pedalling, which will need the guidance of a teacher to help join the harmonies in the very long pedals. Remember, the softer you play the more you involve and draw in the audience. The right-hand chords must be voiced carefully: see *Piano Lessons* Book 3 Chapter 5 for more on chords and balance.

Prelude Op.32 No.5 (Rachmaninoff)

Rachmaninoff was a Russian composer from an old, aristocratic family who became a celebrated pianist, known for his exceptionally large hands and ability to compose the most difficult music. He is best known for his compositions for piano, which are typically highly expressive and lyrical. These works have become the hallmark of every pianist who has the hands to accompany the fiendish compositions. Because this contemplative prelude contains many notes in each bar, it can be difficult to keep the feeling of serenity and smooth, flowing movement throughout the piece. The lyrical right hand should be treated as a song above the accompaniment in the left. The ending floats away – as if in a dream…

PARTITA NO.1

BWV 825

PRELUDE

Johann Sebastian Bach
(1685–1750)

GIGUE

© 2013 by Faber Music Ltd

ALLEGRO IN A

Carl Philipp Emanuel Bach
(1714–1788)

12

SONATA IN F
HOB.16 NO.23
FINALE

Franz Joseph Haydn
(1732–1809)

THEME AND TWELVE VARIATIONS
On 'AH, VOUS DIRAI-JE, MAMAN'
KV265

Wolfgang Amadeus Mozart
(1756–1791)

Variation II

Variation III

Variation VI

Variation XI
Adagio

Variation XII
Allegro

PATHÉTIQUE SONATA
OP.13 NO.8
SECOND MOVEMENT

Ludwig van Beethoven
(1770–1827)

NOCTURNE NO.4 IN A
H.36

John Field
(1782–1837)

SCHERZO IN B FLAT

D.593

Franz Schubert
(1797–1828)

38

D.S. al Scherzo

WALTZ IN B MINOR

OP.69 NO.2

Fryderyk Chopin
(1810–1849)

con Ped.

42

NOCTURNE IN E FLAT

OP.9 NO.2

Fryderyk Chopin
(1810–1849)

TRÄUMEREI
from KINDERSZENEN (SCENES FROM CHILDHOOD) OP.15

Robert Schumann
(1810–1856)

SPRING SONG
from SONGS WITHOUT WORDS OP.62 NO.6

Felix Mendelssohn
(1809–1847)

KINDERSTÜCKE NO.2
OP.72

Felix Mendelssohn
(1809–1847)

Andante sostenuto

OCTOBER (AUTUMN SONG)

from THE SEASONS OP.37B

*The fall, falling down on our poor orchid,
the yellow leaves are flying in the wind.* (Tolstoy)

Pyotr Ilyich Tchaikovsky
(1840–1893)

Andante doloroso e molto cantabile ♩ = c.80

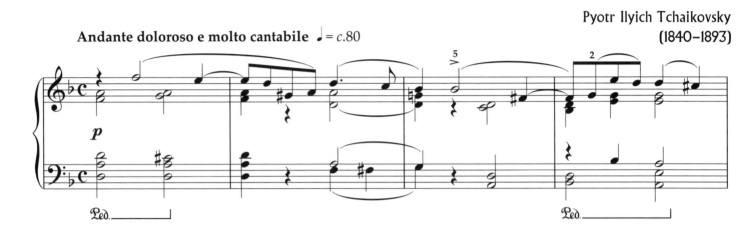

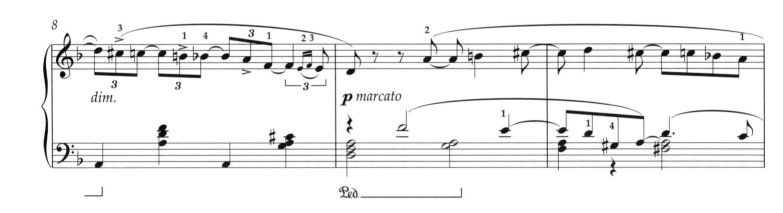

LA FILLE AUX CHEVEUX DE LIN

from PRÉLUDES BOOK 1

Claude Debussy
(1862–1918)

PRELUDE IN G

OP.32 NO.5

Sergei Rachmaninoff
(1873–1943)

© 2013 by Faber Music Ltd
This edition first published in 2013
Bloomsbury House
74–77 Great Russell Street
London WCIB 3DA
Music processed by Jeanne Roberts
Cover design by Kenosha Design
Printed in England by Caligraving Ltd
All rights reserved

ISBNIO: 0-571-53717-0
EANI3: 978-0-571-53717-4

To buy Faber Music publications or to find out about the full range of titles available
please contact your local music retailer or Faber Music sales enquiries:

Faber Music Ltd, Burnt Mill, Elizabeth Way, Harlow CM20 2HX
Tel: +44 (0) 1279 82 89 82   Fax: +44 (0) 1279 82 89 83
sales@fabermusic.com   fabermusicstore.com